Pebble®

I DON'T BULLY

I Am
Trustworthy

by Melissa Higgins

Consulting Editor: Gail Saunders-Smith, PhD

Content Consultant: Susan M. Swearer, PhD
Professor of School Psychology and Licensed
Psychologist; Co-Director, Bullying Research Network
University of Nebraska–Lincoln

CAPSTONE PRESS
a capstone imprint

Pebble Books are published by Capstone Press,
1710 Roe Crest Drive, North Mankato, Minnesota 56003
www.capstonepub.com

Library of Congress Cataloging-in-Publication Data
Higgins, Melissa, 1953–
I am trustworthy / by Melissa Higgins.
pages cm.—(Pebble books. I don't bully)
Summary: "Simple text and full color photographs describe how to be trustworthy, not a
bully"—Provided by publisher.
Includes bibliographical references and index.
Audience: Age 5-8.
Audience: K to grade 3.
ISBN 978-1-4765-4066-5 (library binding)
ISBN 978-1-4765-5170-8 (paperback.)
ISBN 978-1-4765-6035-9 (eBook PDF)
1. Trust—Juvenile literature. 2. Reliability—Juvenile literature. I. Title.
BJ1500.T78H54 2014
179'.9—dc23   2013029991

Note to Parents and Teachers
The I Don't Bully set supports national curriculum standards
for social studies related to people and cultures. This book
describes being trustworthy. The images support early
readers in understanding the text. The repetition of words
and phrases helps early readers learn new words. This book
also introduces early readers to subject-specific vocabulary
words, which are defined in the Glossary section. Early readers
may need assistance to read some words and to use the Table
of Contents, Glossary, Read More, Internet Sites, and Index
sections of the book.

Printed in the United States of America in North Mankato, Minnesota.
092013   007764CGS14

Table of Contents

I Am Honest

You can count
on me.
I'm trustworthy.
I don't bully!

I play by the rules.
Kids who bully
take things
without permission.

I do my own work.
Kids who bully cheat
and ask other people
to cheat.

I tell the truth.
Kids who bully lie.
If I lied, people
would not trust me.

I Can Be Trusted

I keep my promises. Kids who bully only look out for themselves.

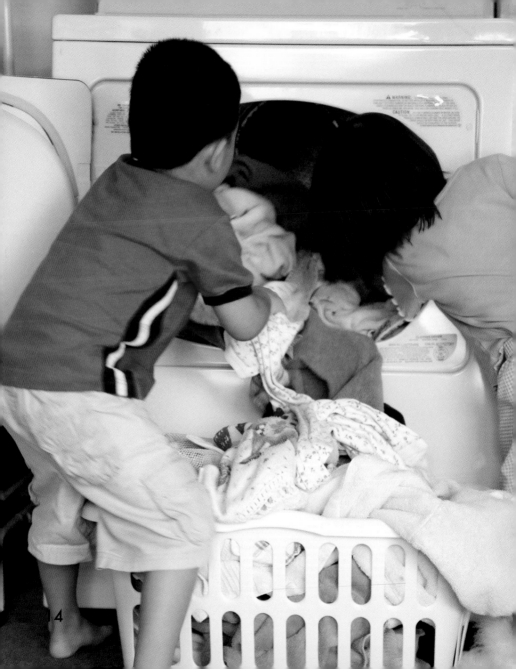

14

I do my fair share.
Kids who bully
take credit for work
they haven't done.

I Am Loyal

I help my friends.
Kids who bully
don't stand up for
their friends.

I can keep secrets.
I only tell adults if
somebody could
get hurt. Bullies share
secrets just to be mean.

I Do the Right Thing

I am trustworthy.
That means I do
what is right.
Bullying is never right.

Glossary

bully—to be mean to someone else over and over again

cheat—acting unfairly to get something you want

credit—praise

permission—the OK to do something

promise—to do what you say you are going to do

trustworthy—can be relied on to be honest and to tell the truth

Read More

Erroll, Mark. *I Am Honest.* Kids of Character. New York: Gareth Stevens, 2011.

Marshall, Shelley. *Molly the Great Tells the Truth.* Character Education with Super Ben and Molly the Great. Berkeley Heights, N.J.: Enslow, 2010.

Meiners, Cheri J. *Be Honest and Tell the Truth.* Learning to Get Along. Minneapolis: Free Spirit Publishing, 2007.

Internet Sites

FactHound offers a safe, fun way to find Internet sites related to this book. All of the sites on FactHound have been researched by our staff.

Here's all you do:

Visit *www.facthound.com*

Type in this code: 9781476540665

Super-cool stuff!

Check out projects, games and lots more at
www.capstonekids.com

Index

Word Count: 127
Grade: 1
Early-Intervention Level: 13

Editorial Credits
Jeni Wittrock, editor; Juliette Peters, designer;
Svetlana Zhurkin, media researcher; Kathy McColley, production specialist;
Sarah Schuette, photo stylist; Marcy Morin, photo scheduler

Photo Credits
Karon Dubke, cover, 4, 6, 8, 10, 12, 16, 18, 20; Shutterstock: Blend Images, 14